M.A Shaheed
B Real
Danielle Dixon
VitaGold
K Kelly

Celebrating!

Larchmere Arts

Album Companion Book

K Kelly McElroy

Celebrating ! Larchmere Arts © 2018 by K Kelly McElroy.

All rights reserved. Printed in the United States of America. No part of this book may be used or reproduced in any manner whatsoever without written permission except in the case of brief quotations embodied in critical articles or reviews.

This book is a work of partial non-fiction. However, names, characters, businesses, organizations, places, events and incidents either are the product of the author's imagination or are used fictitiously. Any resemblance to actual persons, living or dead, events, or locales is entirely coincidental.

For information contact: info@uptownmediaventures.com

Book and Cover design by Team Uptown

ISBN: 978-1-68121-089-6
First Edition: February 2018

10 9 8 7 6 5 4 3 2 1

"This book is Dedicated to all of the people who selflessly drive the culture, that is Black Life!"

K Kelly McElroy

B Real and M.A. Shaheed Performing at Larchmere Arts, Cleveland, Ohio

Vince Robinson playing with band at Larchmere Arts

Table of Contents

Introduction	7
The Poetic Gallery	9
The Beast	11
Chitterling Throne	13
Fictitious	14
Saggin'	16
Amerikka, Girl You Slippin'	17
Mothers	20
My Love Song	22
Black Guilt	25
I Am Fabulous	27
Love Palace	29
Can You?	31

Deliverance	33
True Love	35
I Know	38
The Artists	**41**
M.A. Shaheed	42
B Real	47
Danielle Dixon	49
VitaGold	51
K Kelly	53
Vince Robinson	
The Cultural Advocate	55
About the Author	**59**

K Kelly McElroy

Introduction

Sometimes there are places that have an informal sanctity. A place that certainly does not have the strictures of a church, but expresses spirituality in a way most churches never had or could. After leaving the sanctuary one feels amazingly uplifted. This is how I feel whenever I leave a set at Larchmere Arts. It matters not whether the crowd is large or just a few cats, the vibrant results are invariably positive.

So this book and the accompanying album of the same name is a tribute to one of Cleveland's most important cultural incubators, where new and established artists alike can express themselves absent the strictures of mainstream political correctness. Truth at its purest and rawest form is what brings true spiritual freedom that all good people desire.

Larchmere Arts has hosted events by notable historians and speakers like the renowned Ronoco Rashidi, for example. Larchmere Arts has hosted many culturally and civically relevant people and served as a springboard to their success.

I count Larchmere Arts as a local treasure in the Northeastern, Ohio area. The artists who have contributed to this book and the accompanying album all will attest to this fact, as well. If you are ever in the

Celebrating! Larchmere Arts

Cleveland, Ohio area – we invite you to take a ride on the Mothership! Peace, Joy and Love!

> K Kelly McElroy
> Cleveland, Ohio
> February 4, 2018

K Kelly McElroy

The Poetic Gallery

M.A. Shaheed
- The Beast
- Chitterling Throne
- Fictitious

B Real
- Saggin'
- Amerikka, Girl You Slippin'
- Mothers

Danielle Dixon
- My Love Song
- Black Guilt
- My Torment

VitaGold

    Love Palace

    Can You?

    Deliverance

K Kelly

    True Love

    I Know

K Kelly McElroy

The Beast

(Written by Amirr Rashidd)

Beneath the tall and shadowy trees
My brother black danced with ease
And yet the morning brought disaster
The beast is coming faster, faster.

My brothers black withheld their pride
They went so far as suicide
They surely knew that death held no pains
The beast is coming with shackling chains.

He burned my farm and slashed my arm
And brought me far from home
Across the sea to the land of the free
The beast is coming to burn your home.

The beast said we were ignorant
Said we were totally incompetent
Yes, we won his wars and grew his crops
The beast is coming, your freedom to stop.

Brothers black please hear the cry
Our mothers weep, our fathers sigh
Black men brothers black we're free
Let's fight and die for land you see.

War with the beast, it must be won
The task of fate has now begun
We must strike with such great pain

Celebrating! Larchmere Arts

So that the beast will never rise again.
Brothers black all free men cry
We've won our life through endless plights
Brothers black walk without sigh
The beast is dead, hear freedom cry.

K Kelly McElroy

Chitterling Throne

There they sit, king and queen.
 Keeping the chitterlings clean.
Raising the prince and princess
telling them "it's a culture thing"
on how to respect the chitterling.
How to prepare themselves mentally
to inhale the toilet smells. How
the stuff is full of benefits and a daily
dose of vitamin A. How they must
obey all the rules.

When the debris is cooked and done
 You must hide them in the vegetable
bin just in case some of your folks come in.
Then onhow to
disguise that horrible smell, with air wick
or raid even glade worked well.
Cornbread and coleslaw are the order
of the day it's these two items that keeps the
gout away.

Celebrating! Larchmere Arts

Fictitious

My right to life---Fictitious

My freedom of movement---Fictitious

Rights as a human---Fictitious

My freedom of speech …Fictitious

Lust for blood… Delicious

Having no conscience… Permissive

Equal opportunities --- Fictitious

Justice for all of us---Fictitious

Liberty for all of us---Fictitious

Objective opinions for us---Fictitious

Public opinion---Fictitious

Daily news--- Fictitious

Hollywood movies--- Fictitious

Fair play and balance--- Fictitious
Government for all the people---Fictitious

K Kelly McElroy

Milk of human kindness---Fictitious

Nightly news ---Fictitious

Fixing the environment---Fictitious

Loving thy neighbors---Fictitious

Believing in God... Suspicious?

Saggin'

Saggin laggin behide my brothers and sisters

were lost in time trying to find our place

as a people in a world laced with a plethora

of perverted evils good times equated with sex

and nods from needles / the loudest prayinest people on earth

if we could only wake up cathh up with time and be realize our worth

reverse this cursed state of mind were in

THEE CREATOR made us Gods Goddesses

but we keep wanting to be men and women

undivine deaf dumb and blind to the ways of man kind

saggin laggin braggin about what you aint got

put it to a beat and say thats hot

K Kelly McElroy

Amerikka, Girl You Slippin'

AMERIKA, AMERIKA GOD SHED HIS LIGHT ON THEE...

Amerika one hell of of a place
but you ask GOD shed upon you
THEE Heavenly grace
you kill people you steal people
other countries you lay to waste
you come from evil you breed evil
YOU ARE EVIL!!
the time has come again for you to
LET MY PEOPLE GO
free the peoples minds
from your lies and wicked fairy tales
tell the truth about your roots
so i can overstand why it is i do what i do
i am a product of your enviroment
your CULT-TURE
you are the reason i chase my sisters
your material trinkets like a vulture
is how and american lives
love waxed cold
hate created over the years
taught to love the lies and hate the truth
taught to hate and depsise me
and i look just like you
taught to put on a mask a disguise
dont let your real feelins show through
amerika was built on lies

Celebrating! Larchmere Arts

and thats all babylon will ever produce

Amerika girl you slippin
responsible for the lives of many
you got the people stuck
trying to get the latest gigets and gadgets
your programing marinating the minds
of yours his hers and my kind
you dont obey the ways and customs
of THEE true GOD in the Heavens above
you teach more hate to the children
and show less love
took thy lord out of schools
and replaced THEE with blood
now your the chicken head hoodrat
scurvy punk tramp knuckle head rich broad
enter-tainting the minds with
your tell/lie/vision shows
brothers and sisters going at each others throats
on the tv courts
people putting thier bussiness in the streets
on the jerry springer show
i mean how you gone bring me on national
tell/lie/vision
and tell me this women is a man i been kissin
im bout to catch a case wait.....
no i aint cause i wouldnt even show up. anyway
remeber the murders at the Collinbine school episode
well how many copycats you think would have
followed
if that story was never told
get right girl you slippin

K Kelly McElroy

naked on the beach
plegde ligions to a star spangled banner
is what you preach
what about the convenents we made
family friends my peeps in the streets
i dont care what religion you practice or teach
the covenents pertain to each and every one of us
and our LORD thy GOD is watching every little thing
WE DO
so my people to yourself you got to be true
peace one love from b-real to you

Celebrating! Larchmere Arts

Mothers

MOTHERS MOTHER MOMMIES

HOW I LOVE THEE / LET ME BE REAL AND COUNT THE WAYS
MOTHERS I LOVE YOU NURTURES YOUR CHILDREN
I REMEMBER AS A CHILD MY MOM WARMED MY HEART
WITH OATMEAL KIND WORDS AND HER BEAUTIFUL SMILE
SHE USE TO SAY
"BABY BREAKFAST IS THE MOST IMPORTANT MEAL OF THE DAY"
HER BEAUTY GLOWED INSIDE OUT
SHOWING ME HER SON WHAT LIFE WAS ALL ABOUT
I MEAN MAMA SPIRIT JUST CAME FORTH
LIKE THE COMING OF THE SPRING /BLOSSOMING
ANOTHER RELM GRACEFULLY AGING BLESSDED BY IAM
IT WASNT ALWAYS SMILES AND GOOD WORDS
"I BROUGHT YOU IN THIS WORLD ILL TAKE YOU OUT"
THATS ONE OF THE PHRASES YOU USE TO SHOUT
I CAUGHT A COUPLE OF BOOKS BOOTS AND HIGH HILL SHOES
TO THE BACK OF MY HEAD
HIDING UNDER THE BED SHE HAD HER BABY BOY SCARED
BUT AFTER EVERY WHOOPIN
HER SMILE AND KIND WORDS RETURN

TALKIN BOUT "THAT HURT MAMA JUST AS MUCH AS IT HURT YOU"
BACK THEN I WAS LIKE YEAH RIGHT
BUT NOW THAT I HAVE A SON
I SEE HOW THAT STATEMENT RINGS TRUE
I LOVE MY MOMS FOR ALL SHE DID AND STILL DO
MOTHERS I LOVE YOU REPLENISHERS OF THE EARTH
FOR NINE MONTHS YOU QUEENS CARRY PROPHETS TO BIRTH
RAISING BOYS TO BE MEN AND LITTLE GIRLS TO BE WOMEN
A MOTHERS LOVE UNCONDITIONAL TRUE TILL THE END

I LOVE YOU MOMMIES

My Love Song

My love song ain't dainty
My love song ain't cute
My love song ain't pretty
Cause it's all about that nitty gritty

I don't need your money
You don't need no pickup line
I've already sized you up
So let's stop wastin' time

I ain't got no children
I ain't got no man
I ain't got no worries see
I do just what I damned well please

I party when I want to
I can stay out all night
I ain't gotta check in
And I ain't gotta lie

I ain't no domestic goddess
I wear sweat pants to bed
If you're fine with it I cool with that
If not then I'm still cool with that

I may not put on make up
I may not paint my nails
My love song ain't pretty
It's just all about that nitty gritty

K Kelly McElroy

If you're not too sensitive
  And like to keep it real
Then wear that prophylactic baby
  We can make a deal

No I do not loan out money
I ain't callin' you my man
I ain't tryna meet your mama
Catching feelings would be bad

I ain't gon' be your ride or die
I damned sho ain't your bitch
You're my flavor for tonight
  But tomorrow I might switch

Love me then leave me
I'm tellin' you it's cool
'Cause if you ever stuck around
  You'd be in my way fool

My life is built to suit me
Now, you messin' with my flow
If you can't hang with my speed of life
Then you gon' hafta go

I ain't one of those "New Age" chicks
Sayin' they don't need no man
But truly there's a lot of shit
I've done all by myself

My love song ain't bitter
My love song ain't sweet

Celebrating! Larchmere Arts

My love song ain't witty
But it's all about that nitty gritty

Don't want to diminish
Your value as a man
But if your value's based on what I need
Then sexual healing's what I need

So get in where you fit in
And don't study me too long
If you think about it too hard baby
You gon' learn me wrong

If you're searching for companionship
To keep your life on track
I suggest you run go find her
I ain't tryna hold you back

I will never sweat you for your love
That's just not how I roll
If you need to leave I'm cool with that
If not then I'm still cool with that

My love song ain't cozy
My love does not fall
My love song ain't no love song
     At all.

                                Danielle Dixon
                                Started 2013
                                Revised and finished
                                7/2016

K Kelly McElroy

Black Guilt

I found my long lost brother today
He was waiting for a bus in the rain
He had a look of defeat and disdain
And I didn't want to claim him

So, I covered my face
And tried to push by
But we locked eyes
And I couldn't deny him.

Dirt under his finger nails
Mud on his shoes
Hair unkempt
Sweatin' 80 proof

Asked for a cigarette
Then he asked for a ride
Could I spare a coupla dollars
For a brotha's hard time?

He was running his same ol shit
But I dared not say no
I was already convicted of the crime of
"actin' funny"
In the black court of law.

"It sho' is a blessin' to see you
Out here in this weather
You know us black folks
Gots ta stick tuhgetha"

Celebrating! Larchmere Arts

That's the line he used
To get me to see things his way
But a simple ride around the corner with him
Could commandeer my whole day

A ride to the whiskey store,
the numbers house and something to eat
I wondered if the stench of poverty
Would ever wash clean off my leather seats

So, I apologized
Shrugged my shoulders
Can't help you out today
But my black guilt gave him $50
To make him go away

                    Danielle N Dixon
                    11/5/2017

K Kelly McElroy

I Am Fabulous

I. Am. Fabulous!

I was fabulous 20 years ago
I'll be fabulous 20 years from now
When I'm dead
    I'll be dead and fabulous
I'll be fabulous at 500lbs or 99lbs soaking wet
I'm fabulous when I'm pretty
Being ugly doesn't stop me from being fabulous
I am fabulous in abundance
When I lack resources
    I'm resourcefully fabulous
I was born fabulous
    With the ability to generate fabulousness
My fabulous is a self- contained unit
It morphs, changes, and reinvents itself
    As it sees fit
My fabulous does not need your approval
Yet it remains open to be inspired
    By other people's fabulousness
Because the world needs fabulous people
Playing meek never inspired anyone
And when I see how you wear fabulousness
    Whether you strut it
    Sashay it
    Limp it
    Crutch it
    Or roll it in a wheelchair
I will always applaud it

Celebrating! Larchmere Arts

Because one person's fabulousness does not diminish another's
Fabulousness is infinite
And the world needs your rendition
    Of unapologetic fabulousness
    To be represented
    Right Here
    Right now
    Right where you stand

Danielle Dixon
8/5/2016

K Kelly McElroy

Love Palace

You were the undercurrent of my heart beats a pulse that drove me to that crazy and sad place called love.
My hidden desire a treasure I feared to expose to daylight hours.
Under moonlit nights I fantasized what a world shared only by us would be like.
Would it be all that beautiful running in meadows type shit all hearts and candy land like?
I would soon find it would be none of that. When I presented the key to the beautiful place I built just for you in my heart you said nothing.
Not one word escaped your lips only a look of confusion and a peak over my shoulder at the love palace I created then turned your back on me.
The key still in my trembling fingers I yell for you to come back bewildered as to why you wouldn't want all that my heart could give. Where love once stood rage takes over my love palace turned into a mockery all I see is red and with that I light a match and burn it down to cinders.
The house that my love built lays at my feet turning into a faded memory all dreams shattered and gone past the wind swept away by the torrent of my tears.

Celebrating! Larchmere Arts

The day came when you asked if I was still in love my cynical laugh actually startled you I laughed and laughed until the same tears that once broke my heart were tears of joys at your ignorance.
The moment of clarity you had of realizing all that could have been at your feet laid out like a feast has been buried to the depths of the earth never to return.
Your pain is orgasmic and sublime I love it more than I could ever love you and in it I find comfort in a sick distorted way.
I give a toast to you and without a word I say goodbye to the one who had my heart walking away though in my mind I say fuck you.

K Kelly McElroy

Can You?

Can you write me a tune that resonates through my soul invoking my heart to soar through past the moon into heaven greeting Jehovah to tell him I found the one?
 Can you create a melody that makes my spirit sing and dance in meadows of purple as the wind sings me your name?
Can you bring out the best of me in harmony and jazz tunes my feet tap at the sound of your breath bird land living in my soul because you love me so?
Can you write the words that fall from my lips dripping lyrics of Nina Simone or Billy Holiday I want to dance all day because your love has me high?
Can you bring my heart to life through strife and pain whisper my name and I will fly like butterflies with no destination lost in your cadence?
Can you soothe my soul with the echoes of rhythm and blues your arms wrapped around me like a cocoon this is home?
Sing a song of praise to our love shout it to Allah outside of the most high you are my comfort zone a place to rest when the world outside is a mess you are my love song.
Can you dance with me make me laugh at our rhythm playful like children in the park carefree and

Celebrating! Larchmere Arts

innocent have others join in our play our love is infectious and care free yes please dance with me?
Can you love me when I'm at my weakest give strength and be my better half as I will try to be yours forever until my last breath?
Can you love me the way that I love you our hourglass never running out this is eternal you are me and I you vows that will never be broken?

Deliverance

You are the dream catcher of my soul the light that shines when I speak your name captor of my heart and King of my castle.

You are the reason I breath and wake each day your embrace is warmer than the sun.

You complete me send me to places beyond this world I seek your utterances to fill empty places in my heart.

You are my comfort zone against a cruel world a place of solace and escape I cherish these moments like a woman thirsting for water.

I breath you in like fresh air as you wipe away my tears I was lost until I found you.

I praise you because in your might there is power unknown to wash away my sinful heart and give me peace beyond measure.

Clarity is what I find when I think of you yearning to hold this moment forever as promised I want to be at the right hand of your mercy.

See me beyond my pain and suffering heal me from within so that your glory shines bright for all to see cradle me in your arms and wash away my years of tears.

In you I find shelter a calm from my inner storm torn between this system of things and your will to guide me to life's waters free.

Celebrating! Larchmere Arts

Find favor in me a sinner from birth struggling amongst the blind make my vision clear take away all obstacles I don't want to fight no more.
I am a refugee trying to find shelter take me in and give me favor forgive me I know not what I do.
I turn it all over to you guide my steps as a lantern and let your footsteps show me the way give me solace please I don't want to hurt anymore.
Give me your peace and I will give you my heart the one most deserving becoming the love of my life.

True Love

The word LOVE, so overused and abused
Like the word JAZZ
We don't know where to put non-improvised instrumentals
We're so confused

Truth is, real love is really true
Love is true in the beginning
The end and in between
Everything is everything, and love reigns supreme

This may be true
But – what does it really mean?

Truth is, love is really true
Love is the source of everything in existence
From embryonic creation
To all the wonderful palettes and colors of life

Despite any opposition, it remains persistent
This is true because, love is really true

Love sometimes escapes definition
Yet, a mere child knows in in their heart
Love seeks harmony in its improvisation

Love expresses itself from the spirit and soul
From which it could never part
It's true, because it is
Truly, it's so

Even though true love is truly perfect
It's not always perfectly expressed
Love is the admission of being wrong at times
And throwing pride to the side

It always strives for musical harmony
And always tries its best
For true love is the truth
And wonderfully true it is

It forgives, yet not forgets
For love is not blind
It forgives because negativity and love cannot coexist
It can be done with love because it always strives to be kind

Loving truly, is true love indeed – not just words
If amorous expressions go unrequited
Love still remains, even at a distance
It strives to understand others, and never is spited

True love is truly strong indeed, Truly it is
If hatred, envy, strife or any other negative energy come its way
Love strives for wonder endings, even if dissonant notes are played
Love's dedication to beauty holds sway

Love is simply love
Yes, it is true
Love is far more than just words or even thoughts

K Kelly McElroy

It's what we are

Love can't be selfish
An must look out for the needs of others
Love really is so brilliant and shines brighter than any star

Love is, really love is – it's true
Love can never hate another
Because it understands that all creation is one

Love is eternal, love is real
True love really is true
Because the act of showing true love is never done

As time eternal proceeds
Man certainly must look and pray above
Symphonies of prayers, wishes, wonderment, and questions arise
What would the world be like
If everyone really had – True love…

I Know

Sometimes life can be so unsure
I wonder as I look at the night shy
Sometimes – I'm scared and insecure
Why? – I really wonder why

I remember when I felt on top of the world
It did not seem – that feeling would end
Reality – is sometimes very sobering
I wonder – if I could handle it again

Sometimes, I really… I really don't know

I don't know – what the next hour brings
Don't know – the length of my days
Don't know – if the next time I'll feel real love
Don't know – my creator's ways

I wish – I could peer into the future
Wish – I could tell you for sure
Wish – that all your dreams come true
Wish – that I could make you feel secure

But I know… I really do know

That good things come to those with pure hearts
That spirit lives an eternity
That you can defeat all your fears
That true happiness – can be a reality

One day – it's going to be real

K Kelly McElroy

One day – it's going to be like it should
One day – it's going to be so beautiful
One day – it's going to feel so good

Yes, I know... I really do know

I really know – that real love endures
Really know – when someone's sincere
Really know – I'm going to try
Really know – that God really cares

There are some things that can't be disputed
Yes – some thigs are for sure
No – it's not conditional
What – my feelings are pure

Yes, I know... So what are you going to do?

I know – it's real scary sometimes
Know – you been lied to before
Know - you deserve the very best
Know – you want to have more

Do you know? Do you really, really know?

Do you know – sometimes I'm really scared
Do you know – my heart is really pure
Do you know – real love reigns supreme
Do you know – there's no choice but to endure

Do you know – sometimes dreams do come true
Do you know – there's a hand to catch, when you fall
Do you know – spirit lives an eternity

Celebrating! Larchmere Arts

Do you know – someone hears your call...

I know... I really do know

About The Artists

M.A. Shaheed

B Real

Danielle Dixon

VitaGold

K Kelly

Some members of the Legacies - Channita, B Real and Danielle Dixon

M.A. Shaheed

Mutawaf A. Shaheed writes under the pen name of "C.E. Shy." He had been writing since the seventh grade. After graduating, he worked at the White Motors Company, where he was involved with the company's newspaper. He started a column called: "The Poets Corner," which was his first published work.

He moved to Sweden after he left the "States" with a one way ticket. He met an English photographer and wrote narratives for photographs that would be sold to newspapers and magazines in Europe.

After returning to the States, he joined a poetry workshop, the Muntu Poets, run by the noted master poet and musician Russell Atkins and Norman Jordan, who became an internationally renowned poet himself, from 1966 to 1968. Subsequently, Shaheed became a bassist with the famed Cleveland jazzman Albert Ayler.

He stopped writing for years, but later started back writing again in late 1990's, when he started writing novellas and flash fiction, in addition to poetry. He joined the longest running poetry workshop in Northeast Ohio, at the county library; located in Lyndhurst, Ohio; in 2011 to hone his writing skills. He has been published in several anthologies. His became a co-author in the 1960's with the publication of the *Muntu Poets of Cleveland* anthology of poems, under the tutelage of Russell Atkins and Norman Jordan.

During his hiatus Shaheed married and raised a family. After he recommenced his literary efforts in the 1990's, just like when Miles Davis returned from his sojourn to kick a narcotics habit, he made up for lost time in earnest! Shaheed's published output has been rather prolific considering that he published, in less than three years, over 40 books and counting. He published all those titles with the Cleveland, Ohio publishing house Uptown Media Joint Ventures (http://uptownmediaventures.com).

His literary works under his pen name C.E.Shy include: *Time Share, Substitions, Eclections 2 & 3, Powhims and Proz; The House, Stories - The Long and Short of It Vol. 1 & 2; Me and Maysun, Approaching the Ninth Deminsion; Raw forms, Structures and Vicissitudes of the Neighborhood; Deliver Me From Unconsciousness,*

The Visit, The Door at the End of the Hall, Point Blank! Eclections 4, The Glimpse - A Remote View, A Frayed, Mixed Feelings, Pens and Needles, Five Minutes Pass Midnight, Sketchings, PTSD - Poems That Say Dream, Traveling in the Light, Transparent S, Tuned In, More Questions Than Answers, Balance, If Only I Could, Zero at the End of the Rainbow, Miles To Go While I Weep, Signs and Signals, Watch Out, A Knock On The Door, and *Chapter Z*.

Under Shaheed's oversight, the original *Muntu Poets of Cleveland* anthology of poems was republished in January, 2016. During that same month, the *Muntu Poets – Anthology Volume 2, 47 Years Later with Russell Akins* was published, as well. A remarkable journey that took all the Muntu Poets less than two months to complete from beginning to end.

Shaheed's expressions are not limited to the literary. The resurgence of the Muntu Poets is reflected by several albums of poetry with music that are set for release throughout the year in 2017. The poetry is accompanied by many styles of music including jazz, rap, classical, the blues, EDM, along with many other elements. Shaheed goes by the moniker "Mr. Gentleman," and has completed three albums: *Perspective Now is Then*, *Nomenclature (which was released in 2017)*, and *Point Blank!*

Shaheed has coproduced a documentary short film about the Muntu Poets, *The Muntu Poets Legacy*, which pays due homage to Russell Atkins and Norman Jordan. This film debuted at the Orlando Urban Film Festival on November 12, 2016.

Shaheed is an Imam of a local masjid and a member of a national Muslim (community) (Jaamat,) Called Al Ummah. From 1968 until 1973, he was the head of a very successful prison rehab program that was located in seven prisons in the State of Ohio.

Shaheed has lived in Egypt, Dubai, London, Paris, Stockholm, Sweden. I have spent time in Senegal, Tunisia, Nigeria Trinidad, Guyana, South America Saudi Arabia, Bahrain and Abu Dhabi, and the Artic Circle.

Shaheed's renown has grown by leaps and bounds as he has been invited to speak to various literary, poetry, and educational venues including the NIA Poetry Workshop of the Cleveland Public Library (MLK Branch); the 2016 Men's Adult Literary Discussion Forum of the Cleveland Public Library (Addison Branch); the SUNY (Oneonta) Departments of

Celebrating! Larchmere Arts

History and Africana and Latino Studies, Black History Month Discussion; along with many other entities.

M.A. Shaheed accompanied by many of his books

K Kelly McElroy

B Real

B-Real da poet/musician. Cleveland Born (McDonald House), paralyzed in 1996 in a car accident after being released from prison. He was going through a spiritual war and his prayers led him to poetry.

Twenty years later with, as he puts it, "a clear thought (and peace of mind)," he shares his spiritual growth. The experience "of a man knocked down but not knocked out."

B-Real has performed all over Cleveland including City Hall and the Rock and Roll Hall of Fame. He has performed with the late great Amiri Baraka, he was taught the art of poetry and performed with David (Daveed) Nelson of the *Last Poets*. B-Real prides himself to be counted as one of the *Legacies*, under the tutelage of Cleveland's own *Muntu Poets*.

Celebrating! Larchmere Arts

B Real released a musical spoken word album entitled: *Prayers for My People* in 2017 and continues to be a fixture in the spoken word scene in and around Northeast Ohio and adjoining states.

Danielle Dixon

Danielle Dixon is a local poet and fiction writer from Cleveland Ohio. She got her Bachelor of Art from Kent State University. She has had her poetry published in the *Luna Negra* and *Inclusion Magazine*.

Danielle is an active alumna of the Cleveland School of the Arts where she assists with auditions each spring. Danielle has also been a feature NeoSoulPoet at Larchmere Arts and enjoys getting out to open mic events to test out new work.

Danielle is currently working on a collaboration project entitled: *The Legacy Continues... A Muntu Poet Celebration of the Next Poetic Generation*. and is looking to have a book published in the near future.

Danielle has a musical spoken word album entitled: *Sagittariusly BLUNT!* that was released in 2017.

Celebrating! Larchmere Arts

K Kelly McElroy

VitaGold

Born in Cleveland, raised in New Jersey, VitaGold started writing poetry at the young age of 13. It was like a gift given to her to help her through the difficulties of puberty. Writing poetry for VitaGold was used to cover the pain and woes of life of a young teenager who was raised by her father. During this time, poetry became her passion, which helped sculpt her outlook on life. VitaGold returned back to her home town of Cleveland, Ohio to jump start her career.

In 2010, VitaGold joined the local spoken word scene performing in Cleveland and the surrounding areas. She has performed at several poetry venues like Dreamer's Bar; Grill Writer's Lounge; B Side Lounge; Urban Joe's Cafe - Soulful Expressions; The Stage - Purple Pages; and Club 330 which is located in Akron, Ohio.

Celebrating! Larchmere Arts

VitaGold released a musical spoken word album entitled: *Poetic Reflections* in 2017. VitaGold resides in California and continues to hone her craft.

K Kelly

K Kelly is the proverbial "jack of all trades." He heads a publishing company, Uptown Media Joint Ventures, which has two imprints: Sankofa Freedom Press and Black Pearls. In the meantime he heads Uptown Records which has an imprint, "B Real Records." Along the way he has produced 12 albums over the course of over a year and a half. In the meantime, his desire to express himself poetically has been inspired by the many talents he has been associated with including: Vince Robinson, M.A. Shaheed, B Real, Danielle Dixon, VitaGold, Yaseen Assami, Art Nixon, along with many others.

Vince Robinson

The Cultural Advocate

Vince is the co-owner of Larchmere Arts, a combination photography studio, art gallery and performance venue. There he hosts a bi-weekly spoken word series called NeoSoul Poetry at Larchmere Arts. In August of 2016 and May 2017, he traveled to Ghana, West Africa to film a documentary for Kent State University. The film "The Real Africa" can be seen on YouTube. A collection of photographs from the film has been shown in the Uumbaji Gallery at Kent State University.

Robinson graduated from Kent State University with a Bachelor of Arts Degree, cum laude. He currently co-hosts *360 Info Network*, airing on WERE-AM 1490 Radio in Cleveland and internationally on Black Planet Radio.com. He is also a director, producer, and host of the television program *Open Door* on Cable 9, Spectrum Cable in Summit County, Ohio.

He is the former host of JazzPoetry at the Cleveland Museum of Art, Robin's Nest and Another Level. He currently serves as host of the NeoSoulPoetry Open Mic Series, a spoken word cultural event held in Cleveland, Ohio. An accomplished slam poet, Vince was a member of the Cleveland Poetry Slam Teams that competed in the National Poetry Slam in Chicago (2003) and St. Louis (2004). He has been the featured poet at venues around the state of Ohio.

He is also an author. His first book, *Got Words?*, was published in April, 2015 by Parablist Publishing House, Inc.

Robinson is a public speaker and has appeared at several schools in Cleveland. In January 2001, he was the featured speaker at the Bradley Center, in suburban Pittsburgh, Pennsylvania. He was also the Keynote Speaker for the Jubilee Day Program of the Ross County NAACP in 2016.

Most recently, he was the emcee of the Cleveland Urban League's Men of Distinction Award program (June 2013), which honored television news anchor Leon Bibb of WEWS TV 5, legendary Cleveland Glenville High School coach Ted Ginn Sr., and urologist Dr. Charles Modlin, among others, at John Carroll University.

He has been recognized by Cleveland City Council for promoting literacy and history, working closely with Cleveland City Councilman Kevin Conwell and his band, Vince Robinson & The Jazz Poets. Vince Robinson & The Jazz Poets have been performing in the Cleveland area and other locations in the Midwest since 1997, including the Rock & Roll Hall of Fame and Museum, the Cleveland Museum of Art and others. The group was featured on WVIZ TV25's cultural arts program *Applause* on PBS.

He is a former news reporter for radio stations WERE-AM (Cleveland), WJMO-AM (Cleveland), WHLO-AM (Akron) and WKNT-AM (Kent), producing reports that aired nationally on CBS Radio news. His syndicated radio program *Reflections: A Moment in Music History* aired on stations throughout the state of Ohio with the Ohio Lottery serving as its sponsor.

In addition to radio, he produced and co-hosted *Down to Business*, a television show that aired on WOIO Channel 19 in Cleveland.

A member of the American Federation of Radio and Television Artists, he has been involved the production of documentaries and films and is a voice over announcer. He filmed his first documentary for Wilberforce University in Israel in 1992.

In addition to film projects, Vince is a photo-journalist with credits including Echelon Magazine, Crusader Arts and Entertainment News, Phenomenal Woman Magazine and Cleveland's East Side Daily News. His specialty is jazz photography, with an extensive collection of photographs that include Miles Davis, Ella Fitzgerald, Nancy Wilson and many notable artists dating back to the early eighties.

His photography was also featured internationally on *Comedy from the Caribbean*, a comedy television series filmed in the Bahamas and Jamaica with host A.J. Jamal and guests that included comedians Steve

Celebrating! Larchmere Arts

Harvey and Drew Carey. African American Golf Digest published photographs and an article he wrote on a Panama City, Panama course in 2015.

In addition to his artistic endeavors, Vince is a retired insurance professional. His professional career includes 10 years as a claims representative and 17 years in Risk and Compliance as a reinspector/trainer. He served as co-chair of the Inclusion Advisory Council for State Farm's Mid-America Zone in 2007 and was actively involved in Diversity and Inclusion efforts within the organization.

K Kelly McElroy

About the Author

At the helm of Uptown Media Joint Ventures, K Kelly is following his passion of helping authors get their viable stories published and marketed to their readers! This passion includes expanding the audiences for recording artists and freelance journalists, as well!

K Kelly is an avid Modern Jazz enthusiast. He proudly owns a vintage collection of over 1000 classic jazz CDs. His first jazz book, a buying guide, *Best of the Best Modern Jazz* was an effort to compile his significant knowledge of the genre to assist others who want to develop and enjoy their own modern jazz collection. Modern jazz Classics expands on the concept by adding biographical information for key musicians of the modern jazz era.

K Kelly is the author of the book, *Modern Jazz Classics.* He is a contributor to Original Muntu Poet Robert Fleming's noted work *Free Jazz*, a concise, yet comprehensive, book on the best of modern jazz albums.

Celebrating! Larchmere Arts

K Kelly would like to give thanks all the Original Muntu Poets who have been indispensable in the development of Uptown Media, with special thanks to Russell Atkins, M.A. Shaheed. Art Nixon, Robert Fleming, and Yaseen Assami.

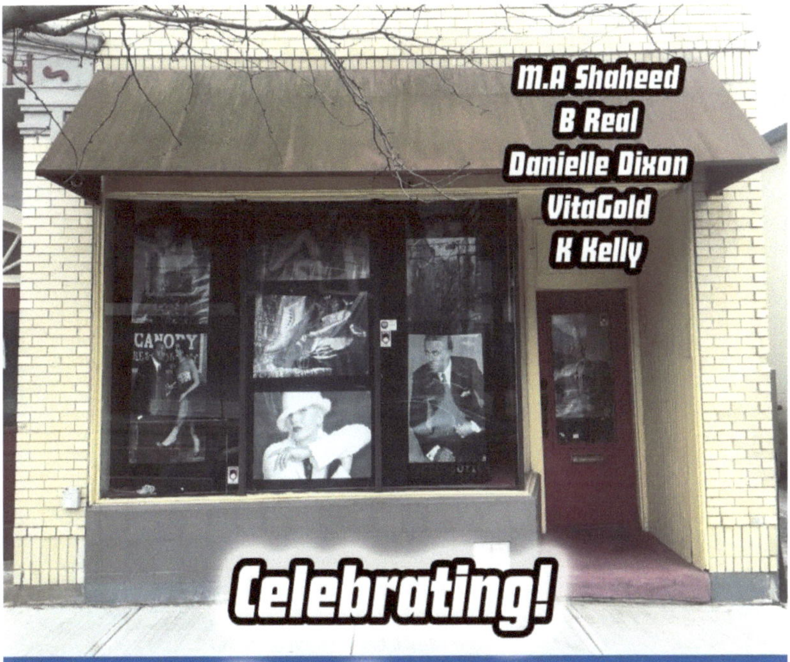

M.A Shaheed
B Real
Danielle Dixon
VitaGold
K Kelly

Celebrating!

Larchmere Arts

Album Companion Book

K Kelly McElroy

www.ingramcontent.com/pod-product-compliance
Lightning Source LLC
LaVergne TN
LVHW010019070426
835507LV00001B/9